Saving

Hilary Walker

Lyndsay,

Best Wishes,

Hilary
x

PreeTa ✳ Press

Foreword

Hilary Walker emerged from nowhere fifteen years ago fully formed as a performance poet with a singular voice, and a clinical selection of phrase and imagery. At least that's my recollection of first seeing her at the legendary Howcroft Inn, then the home of 'Write Out Loud.' She was quite different to others on the circuit and remains so now. Not for her the rant and pant, the machine gun attack, the wail and rail at the injustice of it all. She picks her target or cause and with the greatest of care in choice of word and image, dissects the issue whether it be experiences of motherhood, adolescent mental health, the injustice of government pension policy, with clarity and reason. Her performance graces any stage she is invited to and she has braved the Nuyorican café in New York among many other well-known international venues. She insists on being listened to and to help she makes sure the audience can hear every syllable. Only recently did the penny drop for me when she re-joined the burgeoning North West poetry circuit after a couple of years of putting other things first. As a former registrar of births, marriages and deaths she knows how powerful words can be in helping people through life's significant milestones. But they have to be chosen and delivered with care, treating each one with respect; respect for the word, respect for the subject, respect for the listener. Then she unexpectedly paired her writing and performance skills with husband Paul's jazz piano to finally position herself in the performance world. John Cooper Clark may be Charlie Parker, but Hilary Walker is without doubt Chet Baker, the epitome of cool lyricism and forensically analysed emotion. Buy the book but make every effort to get to see her perform. You won't be disappointed with either.

Dave Morgan

Published in 2018 by
Preeta Press, Bolton, Greater Manchester
preetapress.com
All Rights Reserved
Copyright Hilary Walker

ISBN: 978-1-9998489-4-1

Printed by Printdomain Ltd,

The right of Hilary Walker to be identified as the author of this work has been asserted by her in accordance with Section 77 of the Copyright, Designs and Patents Act 1988.

This book is copyright. Subject to statutory exception and to provisions of relevant collective licensing agreements, no reproduction of any part may take place without the written consent of the author.

Cover design by Paul Blackburn and Hilary Walker

Author photograph by Chrissie Wild

Acknowledgements

Ciorbar with everything featured in Scribble Magazine Autumn 2008 (competition winner)

Bull with a capital B featured in the Wigan Council Magazine, The C E X Files.

Welsh Alec featured in Milestones, the poetry anthology (shortlisted in Write Out Loud Milestone poetry competition) 2017

The Last Nursery Rhyme & Ciorbar with everything featured in Endings, an anthology of works by Skelmersdale Writers' Group 2017

Giving the world to Venus, Traveller, Borderline, Born to be blue & Re-discovering Northern Soul in Australia appeared in various editions of E.C.H.O. Blog/Zine 2017/18

Borderline appeared in an anthology for MIND *Please hear what I'm not saying* edited by Isabelle Kenyon 2018. The poem also features in a video produced & directed by Mark Mace Smith (Thud Dub Films)

Giving the world to Venus & I bring the words appeared in The Fringe Poetry Magazine, Seaquake Publishing 2018

Promised Land appeared on display at the Stratford upon Avon Poetry Festival June 2018 (shortlisted in Peace & Reconciliation poetry competition)

Dedication

For my mother Marion, who gave me the gift of a magical childhood, and my sister, Val for her constant love and support.

The three of us shared a love of literature and a desire to write. There is a joke within our family circle that we are not tactile or demonstrative people, we don't find it easy or natural to hug or throw our arms around one another, instead we write poems.

Additional Quotes …

'In this book Hilary Walker releases a fine collection of her poems which is long overdue. Hilary's poetry is refreshing and delicately written from carefully chosen words taken from her experiences, loves and causes she passionately supports. She delivers her work concisely and thoughtfully but with a hard-hitting edge. It is no wonder she is now a 'must see' poet in demand on the circuit.' Jeff Dawson aka Punk Poet Jeffarama

'Soft and poignant with some real pauses for reflection; Hilary has a habit of blending together words that are carefully crafted from the heart. Dive into this rich collection and allow the thoughts presented to stir up something within you.' Lyndsay Price

Contents

Chameleon of time	1
Promised Land	2
The Disappearing Woman	4
Re-discovering Northern Soul in Australia	6
First Feelings	7
Welsh Alec	8
Conversation with my mother	10
A Suffragette's granddaughter	12
Children in Need	14
Borderline	16
Ridiculously Beautiful Sentiments	18
Traveller	19
The Claim	20
Bull with a Capital B	22
First Love	23
Ciorbar with Everything	24
His next home	27
Coveting Cristina	28
Born to be Blue – Tribute to Chet Baker	30
When you leave me	32
Last Christmas	34
Memories of Central Library Manchester 1972-8	36
Homage to a teen idol	38
The Last Nursery Rhyme	40
I bring the words	42
Woman-o-pause	44
Astrologically Speaking	47
World Cup Winners	47
Giving the world to Venus	48
Every Woman	51

Chameleon of time

I witness the changes to this shell
that is my body

powerless

the pretty plump fullness of long ago
given way to harsher lines,
definition disappeared declined
rounded feminine curves fold into boyish shape
flesh failing,
falling,
surrendering to age
the white flag fills my mirror

occasionally I glimpse my new reflection,
a recent photograph
and I wonder
when did I become so small?

I count the days left to anticipate,
maybe five thousand
or six

these days that come quickly now,
spring turns to winter in a heartbeat

I wrap my arms around each fading dusk and hold on tight
live, I tell myself, live

Promised Land

If all you are guilty of is wanting
a better life for your family

If all you are guilty of is trying not to lose sight
of the light on your children's faces,
as they play among the places
of death and destruction

If all you are guilty of is dreaming
of a past long ago bathed in warmth and laughter,
before the shatter of guns and bombs
replaced the midnight stars with bleeding scars

should you be judged by a stranger from another land
who doesn't take the time to understand
that you, are just like him

when we meet as individuals we learn, we see,
we smile and say 'he's just like me'
we need to sew the seed
and lead every individual by the hand,
one by one, to share our promised land.

If all you expect from your native soil
is war and starvation
wouldn't you summon the determination to walk upon the ocean
to fight, to swim, to pray, to float in motion
across the waves, dreaming,
in search of better days

and if you found yourself drowning deep in condemnation
wouldn't you hope for a little kindness and consideration
along the way
from a stranger who might stop and say

'I understand, take my hand,
come and share our promised land.'

The Disappearing Woman

Can you see me? Am I here?
I have a tendency to disappear
To fade away before your eyes
I'm a sexagenarian female –it's what we do, it's no surprise

Ok, so maybe I'm not the woman I was
or, maybe I'm the woman I am because
of the years that live in the lines on my face
in the re-shaping of my body
and my place in the race
but why should I succumb to the expected agenda
just because it's autumn, my October, my nearly November

'Autumn paints in colours that summer has never seen'

My opinion is immaterial, invisible, disposable
an age-old policy - non-negotiable
I'm supposed to go gentle into my journey of decline, to re-align,
to have the presence of mind to resign from the frontline

News Headline: Shock, horror at the age of 63
Dame Helen Mirren dares to wear a bikini!!!

In this world where media rules us
I'm portrayed either as a smiling grandma or a groping cougar

I'm one of the disappearing women, slip-sliding away
we're lost, ignored, unnoticed,
a greying, decaying product of yesterday
and if, God forbid,
we have the temerity to look good,
then we look good – for our age
we're doing great – for our age
we look fab – for our age

Well hey - turn the page, lets engage, rage, rage

At my age, I still think
At my age, I still dream
At my age, I still lust
At my age, I still feel
At my age, I still hope
At my age, I still love
I'm still here, I didn't disappear
and I look good……… end of sentence.

Re-discovering Northern Soul in Australia

Men pushing sixty
dragging their almost 'zimmered' limbs
single-mindedly
'out on the floor tonight, we're really movin'

Nostalgia, the drug of the future,
and we're pumped,
legally high on memory while
'the beat is runnin' right'

Smell those clandestine overnighters
taste the sweet kookaburra of youth
that meant nothing then and the world now,
time waits for no woman.

And the place is packed with Brits
who've settled;
'bloody good down under mate'
but no-one wants to die so far away from home

So they *'keep the faith'*
'long after tonight is all over'
long after it's all gone
tender illusions of memory recreate the
glitter-ball of our sad collective mind

Wigan Casino died,
its southern soul is alive and
high kicking in Freemantle, Western Australia
third Friday of the month,
7.30pm start,

bring your best moves,
it's a long dance home.

First Feelings
(for my wedding day 2005)

I don't remember the moment I met you,
which is rare for someone like me
I usually recall the date clearly,
along with the weather, and what was for tea.

I could say it was instant attraction,
but it didn't quite happen that way,
more of a passionate, but comfortable, newness
while real life and stuff, got in the way

But I do remember the first feeling,
it was like reaching my destination, safe and warm,
call it fate, call it kismet, call it magic,
or just finding my way, home

Welsh Alec

He was one of those people who grew better looking with age, time was a friend,
snow-white hair, favourite pink shirt, distinguished, debonair,
Welsh Alec, a poor man's David Niven

'He doesn't take life seriously' my sister and I worried
'look at the state of the house now, it's falling down'
but my father had other gifts to share

Gregarious, flirtatious and sociable, at ease with his light-hearted life,
his 'piece de résistance' was dancing,
a smooth foxtrot, a nimble quick-step, an elegant waltz
and the women came in droves:
Betty, Sally, Alice, lovely Alice, Jean, Vera, Miriam, Joan, nightmare Joan,
my father was a widow's dream, his little black book overflowed

We danced through my childhood together,
cocooned in a safe world of MGM make-believe
and long-limbed dancers on a black and white screen:
Rita Heyworth, Cyd Charisse, Ann Miller
and my father, a poor man's Fred Astaire

'Tell me about Wales, Dad'
though I knew the stories off by heart:
running over the mountain to school
midnight poaching with his Dad
the poverty,
the strike that led to leaving the valley to move up north
losing his accent so he wouldn't be teased
and teaching his children to say
'llanfairpwllgwyngyllgogery-chwyrndrobwllllantysiliogogogoch'

Later came wartime tales of North Africa, Italy and Salerno
no bad memories shared,
camaraderie, good times and the humour of his pals:
discovering melons in Alexandria
going AWOL for mum's birthday,
witnessing that Glenn Miller concert,
a poor man's John Mills

All this and the early death of
his own Ginger Rogers –
so Welsh Alec made a choice to enjoy life,
to keep it light
'bugger the house' he'd say 'let's go dancing'
When he died my sister and I worked
through his little black book,
the women came to his funeral in droves,
sad-eyed widows, and married ladies
lingering in the shadow of gravestones

my father taught me to dance the foxtrot,
and so much more.

Conversation with my mother

People play a game: 'who would you invite to dinner,
dead or alive, saint or sinner'
impress with guests like
Mandela, Marilyn maybe Madonna

For me, I would only wish to see one name on the list,
my mother's

Memories are childlike
for I was always a child with her.
Now we'd meet through adult eyes for the first time and
I'd learn so much about the woman who changed everything

Recollections are sweet:
exotic skin, quick to darken in meagre sunlight,
the touch of soft flesh on her arms as we'd link each other,
mother and child sharing secrets, laughing in tandem
her serenity,
her scent,
how safe it was, my home within the centre of her world

Over dinner I'd ask her why,
why she suffered so much,
why she didn't tell, see a doctor, left it too late
and I would lie and sensitively say,
that I don't really remember her in that way

Haunted by questions:
If she had lived, who would I be
If she had lived, whose life would I be living
A part of me is buried beside her, for children always blame themselves

There is no resemblance but lately, amazingly,
I learned a magical truth that warmed my soul

My mother loved to write!

Throughout my adult life I've been fine,
for most of the time
but today I am frozen
finally realising how much I lost.

A Suffragette's granddaughter
(Poem for the WASPI Campaign – Women Against State Pension Inequality)

I'm a suffragette's granddaughter and a WASPI Woman
1950's born, working class and some say stubborn
and although my grandmother's generation
managed to attain such wonderful heights
twentieth century women still had to fight, for what was right
to fight for equal payment, to fight to join pension schemes
to fight for work around childcare, to achieve any of our dreams

We've worked hard, raised families,
cared for parents and paid into our pension
But the government of the day changed the rules, at short notice
without a word, without barely a mention
and when we said 'but no-one told us' Mr. Opperman suggests
we take an apprenticeship and stop having a moan,
but I ask you, forty-six thousand pounds adrift
and they informed us, condescendingly, via an advert in
Woman's Own!

And George Osborne's boast of how cheating us was 'easy money',
was expected to be ignored
they assumed our generation would accept the situation
they assumed we'd go away and do as we're told, because we're old
but we're not suggesting we change the rules
we're not suggesting we retire at sixty when men work until sixty-five

we support equality for men and women,
we just needed to be told in plenty of time

There are aging women struggling with manual work
There are aging women dependent on food banks & charity
There are aging women suffering alone in silence
they deserve a little respect and a lot more clarity
So here we are in limbo, no money, no jobs, growing older, no retirement plans
campaigning for fair arrangements, asking the government to listen,
to hear our demands, to understand
until they do, one thing is certain, like the suffragettes before us, we're not going away,
until we receive that fair hearing, until we receive justice,
WASPI women are strong and united, WASPI women are here to stay.

Children in Need

When my child was in need I asked *Children in Need* for help

'Sorry' they said 'we only help recognised, diagnosed, pre-determined, pre-disposed, medically chosen children in need at Children in Need, would you like to donate some of your pay, or maybe come back another day.'

When my child was in need I asked the doctor for help.

'Sorry' he said 'your child needs counselling but there's a waiting list, she might grow out of it one day' he dismissed,
'would you like to pay or maybe come back another day.'

When my child was in need the teacher sent for me every day

'Sorry' she said 'your child is dangerous, contagious, her behaviour is outrageous,
we'll have to exclude her today, she can't come back another day.'

When my child was in need I asked social services for help

'Sorry' they said 'you adopted her, she's your problem, go home and be a good mother or we'll write a report about you today.'

When my child was in need the policeman came

'Sorry' he said 'your child is carrying knives, she's threatening other children's lives, she'll go to prison one day if she carries on in this way.'

When my child was in need and attempted to take her own life the psychiatrist came

'Sorry' she said 'but you need to give up caring, stop helping her, stop despairing, take a step away and say I can't do anymore for her today.'

On another day, years and years away, when my child was no longer a child, she finally became needy enough for help.

Please help children in need!

Borderline

We are as one
my damaged girl and me,
drowning deep within her constant need
and my unrelenting sense of responsibility

She has two thoughts, black and white
She has two emotions, love and hate
She has two judgements, goodness and evil
there is no middle ground, they call it borderline

and we live on the border of life,
like refugees in our own diminished detention centre
waiting indefinitely for good news, for normality, for acceptance

while we wait I learn the language of our new world
but the words all sound the same
psychology psychotherapy, psychotic, psychosis

she waits desperately,
chronic intensity raging raw against invisible walls,
cutting to cope, for a sense of hope
cutting to release, for a promise of peace
cutting to feel, cutting to heal
cutting to breathe, cutting to believe
cutting to survive, cutting to stay alive

abandonment - her worst fear,
the all too familiar mantra sounding loud and clear, in my ear:
I hate you, please don't leave me

I have more than two thoughts
I have a million, and then a million more,
they litter the floor, they hide behind the door,
they shout, they scream, they whisper, they roar
One more dance with the devil
One more midnight deal with god
One more last chance
One more…

They tell me I'm now a Carer, but some days I don't care anymore

but we are as one
my damaged girl and me
for the scars that cover her body
bleed deep into my heart

Ridiculously Beautiful Sentiments

Crawling in beside me in the early hours
late night affection showered,
whispered reflections of our lives fall away.

I'm too tired to listen
lingering in that half-land of wakefulness,
on the brink of slumber
missing his unencumbered thoughts.

Ridiculously beautiful sentiments pass me by
invisibly caressing my mind
and though I try hard to murmur a tangible reply
sleep claims me,
creeping up to hold us still, into the night

Until tomorrow or the next day when I'm busy with life
and then I remember
a buried phrase of tenderness
a moment of silent togetherness
a warmth unlike any other
and I know what it is to be loved.

Traveller

To experience - you say,
to explore another culture or maybe to find yourself,

Is that why India called?
You ride her trains with privilege, peer at her world through first class eyes and
wrinkle your nose at the smell of poverty.

On the platform the beggar speaks in English
'I have no money and must go home, will you give it to me?'

The ragged child taps your arm as another reaches inside your bag.

But India sings to you,
offers herself to your imagination as she attacks your senses,
punches you deep into her colours,
her aroma,
her spices,
her noise,
her dirt,
her heat,
all staining your soul.

Then you visit the mausoleum, the reason you travelled so far,
Crown Palace of love and beauty,

and as the sun gloriously rises above the Taj Mahal

you find your breath
and your words are silently swept away.

The Claim

In Ranthambore in spring we came to find her,
elusive Bengal Tiger
ancient Royal hunting ground now protecting,
restoring her natural habitat and environment.

Late last afternoon safari,
six to a jeep, into the thick bush of sector number two,
enthusiasm excitedly carrying hopes.

We dust and bump over challenging Jurassic terrain
passing by tiger fodder:
blue bull antelopes, Indian gazelle
and monkeys calling to us, a mongoose, woodpeckers
and wild peacocks

At times we'd stop, kill the engine to hear our silence,
collectively holding our breath,
passing by jeeps, exchanging smiles with fellow cat seekers,
hiding the thought 'will I be lucky, or will you?'

Then a radio message and a whoop of determination,
we race hard, holding on tight, hearts pounding,
exuberance mounting.

We slam on the brakes, cameras click, a video switch at the ready
jostling for position in the jeep 'where, where'
and suddenly, in the distance - she is there.

A tigress, big and full,
bold and majestic striding slowly and with such purpose
through the clearing.
Noisy animals shriek their warnings,
fellow travellers whisper in awe,
jeeps arrive quickly, loudly, in abundance, but too late.

My eyes hold onto her as she fades away,
the moment, so fast, sweet and full of wonder now gone.

Disappointed latecomers look on in envy
and glimpse only the smugness of our face.
We were all brash and triumphant,
unashamed to make our claim for she chose to reveal herself to us,
she was our tiger,
we owned her if only for a brief moment in time.

Bull with a capital B

Email to all members of the D.M.T.
our esteemed leader, the D.C.E
kindly requests your company
at today's team briefing to be held at three
rescheduled at short notice to committee room B
followed by the usual refreshments of biscuits and tea
and for those of you with vegetarian needs, dietary
see Penelope, the temporary interim secretary
to the Assistant Deputy, D.C.E.

Now it is the D.C.E.'s current aim you will see
to extend to his loyal, incentivised employees
the distinct and rare opportunity
to raise issues of extreme delicacy
pertaining to the general feeling of discrepancy
whilst brainstorming ideas of diversity
given today's climate of awareness and equality
within the expected boundaries of recognised integrity

You see, the D.C.E., particularly,
feels it's essential, initially
to advise staff in fairness and all honesty
regardless of the traditional view departmentally
to explain, in depth, somewhat systematically
the relative information to be delivered, cascadingly
under the umbrella of projected vision now quite obviously
limited with the proactive training given, disproportionately
fast-forwarded to the development of recycled technology
incorporating experience and maturity, automatically
allowing for the flourish of graduated youthful authenticity

motivating corporate good practice, dispassionately
responsively leading towards marketing trends, alarmingly
flagging up the need for structure and benchmarking harmony

And finally, the D.C.E. welcomes your comments, objectively
taking the helicopter view, 'out of the box' respectively
requesting any team member unable to attend, disappointedly
to forward the usual sincere heartfelt grovelling apology
for your absence will be noted, regrettably
and your future may be amended, accordingly

First Love

Summer 1975
10cc *I'm not in love*
Stamford Park Boating Lake
You were harder to remove from my heart
than the grass stains on my skirt.

Ciorbar with everything

Her name in Russian meant 'Little Doll',
Puca,
Now, in middle years,
her Doll like features danced across her face
when she smiled

In this alien existence Puca was my light,
she was my welcome
she was my warmth

sit, sit, sit, eat, eat, eat
small English words she was confident with.
She gesticulated wildly bringing out plate after plate
of old, cold meat, bottles of preserves and to begin,
always was Ciorbar

It was a kind of soup,
Red
Extract of beetroot
Lukewarm
Harsh,
Bitter
And very obviously with something missing

She'd stand over me as I ate, watching, anxious

I always began with gusto, not wishing to offend

'I'm full honestly, Puca,
I'm just not very hungry today'
I'd mime all my weak excuses.

Doll like features would crumple
So, I'd force down a few more spoonfuls

It was post revolution Bucharest
post normality
post lack of food
Radu, her husband, shot dead for daring to speak out

His widow believed that life would get better now,
She had to believe, but when? and how?
so she kept busy, making *ciorbar* with everything.
Months later she came to stay
'Little Doll' in England
Puca saw Sainsbury's and wept
'such choice, such choice'

She bought fresh herbs and fine quality ingredients
and in my well stocked modern western world kitchen
Puca made ciorbar for me

It was a kind of soup,
Red
Extract of beetroot
Lukewarm
Harsh
Bitter

And very obviously with something missing
She stood over me watching, anxious

I ate with gusto, all of it
Smiling, laughing
Doll like features beamed

Her name in Russian meant 'Little Doll'
and nothing to do with being a good cook.

His next Home

He arrives without expectation, wary, questioning:
is there Wi-Fi?
his favourite cereal?

Family number nine, new house rules,
all over again
the tattered box of memories is hidden, out of sight,
under the bed,
in time he might share photographs of far-away family,
he settles slowly,
begins to fit in.

You watch with sadness as his mother's new baby is taken away,
he asks you why and you cannot judge,
this mother who he loves unconditionally
one day begins to topple from the peaks of his highest pedestal,
you listen when the pain of realisation finally hits home

why did she let him down, again?

You care for him,
include,
encourage,
make him laugh,
build confidence,
challenge views,
give hope,
dare him to dream,
such small steps,
it doesn't feel enough,
maybe one day it will make a difference

Coveting Cristina

There was a space in time when Cristina was mine
though we never met

the new spring day matched my mood
alluded the same bright attitude of anticipation,
longed for thoughts of motherhood swarming my mind

'a baby girl' he'd said, 'only three months old' he'd said
'in perfect health, no need to visit the orphanage'
a daughter available to adopt in this torn land of revolutionaries

and hadn't I seen the baby boy he'd found for another desperate lady,
a dream already materialised, my own happy ending realised in my head

we left the foreign city behind
journeyed through villages where time had remained the same

inside the parlour of a farmhouse we perched on high backed chairs
kept for best,
a glass of something to be hospitable, overblown gestures mimed,
a nervous smile, a knowing nod

Holy Icons of Christ bore down on me
as Cristina's grandfather bargained in a foreign tongue,
a ritual of waiting and wondering if something was wrong, or not

I never met her, but I heard her cry
before the piercing scream of her mother
as they wrenched her from her arms,
before I learned they were offering me a wanted child
a much loved and desired child,
a baby for sale to the highest bidder,
small matter the love her young mother had to give her

the baby-seller whispered his persuasion in my ear
'this mother is in complete agreement to the adoption,
but baby Cristina is so beautiful she cannot bare to part,
though in her heart she is determined to give her to you'

'No' I replied, 'no, no, no, no'
'I want a baby but I'm not a monster and I would rather give this
mother everything I have before I'd steal her baby,
shame on you,
shame on you'

We travelled back to Bucharest in silence
Sadness stilling my mind, killing my silly mummy dreams
Sadness for Cristina and her mother, as monsters would come
one day

Years later, I'm haunted by hindsight
should I have taken her,
and saved her,
and saved me,
and kept her safe for her mother
though we never met there was a space in time
when Cristina was mine.

Born to be blue – Tribute to Chet Baker
(Performed to a piano version of *My Funny Valentine*)

Rebel with a horn, Oklahoma born
trumpet player, giant song slayer
Oh, how you lived, no safe path for you
jazz maker, born to be blue

The one and only funny valentine
velvet tone pleading, please be mine,
makes me cry with each innocent sigh
vulnerable, effortless
incomparable, tenderness

A style icon, hypnotic, haunting sound
James Dean Cool, the Prince was crowned
and all the chicks would hang around,
wanting you the most - 'the little white cat on the coast'

You sang 'Let's get lost in each other's arms'
'Time after time' full of charm
'Just Friends'- the magic never ends
chance taker, cool cat – you

but bad boy junkie, wasted life,
faceless women, lovers, wives
wounded, withered, battered, beaten,
promises broken, West of Eden

Far too soon, too early, self-destruction won
a push or a fall and the bad boy was gone,
in a corner of Amsterdam a plaque sadly proclaims
your dying place,
a picture of your ravaged face
a shrine to a different time
when you were born to be blue

What's left is the music,
Pacific jazz, west coast sound and glory
reborn with each new generation
falling in love with your story
subtle tones, velvet voice,
sweet trumpet moans, perfect choice
jazz maker, chance taker, Chet Baker,
born to be blue

When you leave me
(Performed to Dawn by Dario Marianelli, from the film Pride & Prejudice 2005)

When you leave me, as you will,
don't desert me for a casual fling
some sad hidden one-night stand that you will say
meant nothing

If you leave me, when you do
don't compromise or tell me lies
leave me guessing, questioning everything,
who you've spoken to, who you've seen
and don't tempt me into checking messages on your phone,
smelling invisible perfume on your clothes when you come home,
don't turn me into the crazy lady
who empties your pockets when I'm all alone

Leave me if you must, but if you really must
then leave me for her, the woman of your dreams:
for the one who makes you feel tongue-tied and stupid
at the same time as knowing you can never live without her
for the lover who makes your heart beat faster, who has that
'special something' to last a lifetime

Leave me for the future mother of your children,
for the perfect lover,
for the one who makes you feel alive and is the reason
you could never love another

For the woman who gives you everything you could
possibly need,
the woman who makes you the best man you can ever be

So,
 leave me to play Mr. Darcy to your Elizabeth Bennett,
your grand passion,
your soul mate
and the one who occupies your thoughts
each and every single minute

Only leave me for the very best,
for the woman who is simply, enough
then, maybe, possibly, one day
years from now I'll understand and give you my blessing.

Last Christmas
(Performed to a piano version of *Have Yourself A Merry Little Christmas*)

Her last Christmas was spent suspended
between the living and the dying
in a place where they called her by a different name

On good days she knew she was dwindling
on bad days she didn't care,
even when the monster crane
hoisted her tiny frame

It was a different sort of life now
for the liberal lady with the enquiring mind:

disposable bibs to catch the dribbles
incontinence pads regularly checked
dignity firmly diminished

Her nephew comes to visit,
over mince pies and a glass of sherry once again she hears her name

'The care home has three stars Auntie Babs, and the gardens are lovely'
'Merry Christmas, all the best, Auntie Babs.'

The staff were mostly kind
'Are you in pain, my love'
they ask all the time.

Her turkey dinner is served pureed, a spoon-fed dance
between carer and patient

Voices ring out, choirs singing Christmas Carols and the memories
flood her mind:

Her husband
Her little dog
Her golden days

'Tomorrow is Festive Bingo Barbara' she hears
'and you can have your hair done, you'll like that'

She reaches for her purse and
presses a coin into the palm of her favourite nurse
'Happy Christmas my love' she whispers, 'God bless'

Memories of Central Library Manchester 1972-78

This is my place of education
of hurried lunchtimes buried in the history section,
ten spare minutes before the bus
to squeeze an extra paragraph or two
from Catherine the Great's biography
or the story of cartography

This is my place of teaching
my reaching out for hidden potential,
a welcome from the wasteland of eleven plus failure
the saviour of an average plodder
destined for mediocrity

This is my place of discovery
the haven where I found poetry,
words reborn with deeper meaning,
a world of dreaming in a language of long ago.
Why didn't anyone tell me?
Shakespeare, Byron and Browning,
newer names like Larkin and Cope
and Emily Dickinson's description of hope, inspiring me

This is my place of wonder
a magical dome of peace and stillness
where knowledge is free,
amazingly, they will let me
take nine books home
nine beautiful hard-backed lessons loaned.

This is my place of comfort
where I can retreat inside books that teach me about life.
Allow me to breathe in the past
away from lovers breaking my heart
and taking part in office gossip,
indulging the wine bar mentality

This is my place of history
my time-travelling days of revolutionaries,
where I met with Russian royalty
and fell in love with renaissance beauty
Studied Civil Wars in England and the USA,
discovered Leonardo and all he had to say,
art and paintings came alive to me
along with everything else they didn't teach in 5C.

This is my place of performance,
a space of enormous affection
This is my place of reference,
devoured section after section
This is my university,
This is so much more than a library to me.

Homage to a teen idol

You and me
and the secret plans we made together
in my bedroom in 1973
Could it be forever

You and me
and the songs you sang
achingly wistful
serenading my teenage dreams
I woke up in love this morning

You and me
your name etched on my pencil case:
your favourite colour
your star-sign
your middle name
Cherish

You and me
Jackie magazine,
where 'Cathy and Claire' share all the answers
first crush, first concert, first love
Daydreamer

You and me
and thousands of others just like me
learnt you weren't exclusive
learnt to grow up
learnt that
Breaking up is hard to do

You and me
David Cassidy
the memories, the moments
the time when I planned to change my world
as you looked down from the poster on my wall,
sending me
The Last Kiss

R.I.P.

The Last Nursery Rhyme

In the summer of 1964
the bogeyman came to town
don't talk to strangers
don't accept sweets
my mother's rhetoric drummed into my sensible little head

The Hillman Hunter was sky-blue,
my favourite colour,
boyish good looks
a relaxed smile
no warnings

He asked questions and I replied,
polite little girl
good little girl
curious little girl

until the moment he reached for me
whispering the words,
new words
strange words
bad words

and so I ran,

fast, in my ankle socks and navy blue buckled sandals,
fast, in my green gingham summer school dress
fast, with my pony tail and ribbons flying in the wind
fast, as my innocence could carry me

from the safety of the school yard
behind the grey peeled painted railings I watched

his menacing stare
the threatening wave
an evil blown kiss
as he casually drove away

three times I tried to tell Miss but I couldn't say the words,
and somewhere deep inside I recognized a feeling,
maybe I'd done something wrong,
maybe it was all my fault

he hadn't hurt me, but the world had changed.

I bring the words (the work of a funeral celebrant)

I bring the words for the departed and the dead
I bring the words to say who he was,
what she did, and what they said

I bring the words
with dignity, to signify their worth, words to describe a space in time,
a human lifetime from birth

I bring the words
I talk of times when life was new,
reflected in hearts and minds
stories to keep the memories alive

I bring the words
I place them in order, in ways that matter to shattered lives,
when someone dies

I bring the words
I give them time, words bathed in light and laughter,
words to hold onto forever after

I bring the words
spirituality for the bereaved, bereft
humility, humanity, a non-religious Christianity

I bring the words when there is no-one to mourn,
no-one to hear of a past glorified, no life sanctified

I bring the words when there are no words,
no words to heal,
no words to feel we make a difference

I bring the words for everyone
the rich, the poor, the old, the young
words that don't differentiate, dying doesn't differentiate

I bring the words to end the journey,
to say farewell, to bid goodnight
I bring the words for life's finale, words for the closing of the light.

Woman-o-pause

I'm hot flushing,
blushing from breakfast until the early hours,
a wilting flower,
and all through the night
I'm sweating,
radiating heat,
deprived of sleep,
kicking off the sheet
until I surrender and creep
into the spare room, to wallow in my oasis of gloom

I'm hot stuff,
literally,
embarrassingly
toe curling,
crawl into a ball and stay at home preferring,
because this malaise is confidence draining,
self-esteem waning
negativity staining

In my mother's day it was called 'the change',
whispered about as if to be ashamed,
and to some its still a stereotypical joke, but would it be so funny
if it happened to your average middle-aged bloke?

I'm bodice ripping,
stripping
get these clothes off me now
dripping, with perspiration
spilling, my hot tears of frustration

And I've tried all the remedies,
the solutions,
the supplements,
spent a fortune on herbal and natural accompaniments,
from HRT,
vitamin E,
acupuncture,
hypnosis to red clover,
clonidine,
wild yam cream,
soya,
sage, and other stuff bought over
the counter and the net,

and let's not forget –
the lady garden magnet,
discreetly positioned in your underwear,
to re-balance your hormones but ladies, take care,
you don't want to look like a total wally
when you're shopping in Aldi, attached to your trolley!
.
I'm steaming, dreaming of days without visible gleaming,
I'm smoking, a personal towering inferno, no joking,
I'm shining, moist with terrible timing
I'm stifling, damp and depressed over something so trifling
I'm burning, yearning for a cure so I won't have to endure,
I'm boiling, hot, not the most attractive feature I've got
I'm glistening, trying to find a way but no-one's listening
I'm on fire, cooking without libido or desire

But what might make me feel just a tiny bit better
is to own this condition, re-arrange a few letters
It's time to claim and rename this men-o-pause
it's a feminine phenomenon, it's a female lost cause,
so shout out, ditch the shame, let's have a round of applause,
for at the very least it ought to be known as the 'woman-o-pause'

Astrologically Speaking

His rising sign
was the same as mine
but he had Mars in lager
and I had Venus in wine.

World Cup Winners

2002 South Korea/Japan
black eye

2006 Germany
punched in the face, bruises, and burns

2010 South Africa
rape, broken collarbone

2014 Brazil
ruptured spleen, hospitalised for four days,

2018 Russia
I will leave him

Domestic Violence increases 25% during England World Cup matches.

Giving the world to Venus

Row upon row, cot upon cot,
and the smell.

I watch the worn out, tired, hard-life women
as they casually throw babies around for a living,
they hold a child, feet first under a freezing cold water tap
and grin with amusement to see my horror at that.
It's hard not to judge

Babies for sale, dark-skin cheaper than pale,
babies damaged, derailed,
babies with missing years lost inside their heads as they rock,
and rock

Children paraded, tiny hands reach out to grab hold of my heart,
two years old but babies,
undersized, unsteady, undernourished
and some already looking at life through empty eyes

a voice says
'We don't wish to offend but would you be willing to
consider a gypsy child?'
It's hard not to judge

My gypsy baby is number twelve,
she is the smallest and the darkest,
but her eyes shine and tell me she is still holding on tight to her
spirit,
no sign yet of surrender

I hold this tiny life and ask myself what right I have
to take her from her country, her culture and her creed,
then I look around at her country, her culture and her creed
and know for certain that she will die here,
even if she lives,
so I'm sold, and I'm told I must find her mother,
find Venus

Venus with her rich olive skin is beautiful
but Venus is not the Goddess of Love,

Venus is young and has no shoes
and snow is falling lightly above the filthy oil fields of Prahova County.

We smile and I try to remember everything.
I'm told she has dreams for the baby she's never seen,
to become an English princess, like the daughter of a queen.
It's hard not to judge

I want to buy Venus some shoes
but the interpreter scorns and warns
'She's just a gypsy, she'll want more,
you must show her you are strong'

But I don't want to be strong,
I want to give her the world for she has given the world to me.

Rebellion kicks in
Venus and I link arms and go shopping in downtown Bucharest.
In department stores devoid of light we rummage together cheerfully,
new comrades searching deep in the darkness

We emerge triumphant with an odd pair of ill-fitting boots,
and as I raise my eyes to gaze at the mother of my child,
I see Venus, the Goddess of love,
who now stands magnificently with the world at her feet.

Every Woman

I am her
every woman who lost the innocence of childhood
at the end of a hospital corridor.
every woman who married believing she would find the answers
achieving
someone else's dreams.

I am she
every woman who has clung to a dying relationship
long after instinct and tears recognised insecurities and fears.
every woman who has cried at the unfairness of infertility,
screaming at the world 'why me' reluctantly accepting what
others dispassionately say 'was meant to be.'

I am me
every woman who has been betrayed and stayed
to give him another chance to dance to our song.
every woman who is ashamed to admit she's been the betrayer
too,
made excuses for straying instead of communicating her needs,
expressing her seeds of doubt.

I am her
every woman who has wanted to be thinner,
promising herself that life would begin again if only she were a
size ten.
every woman who has looked in the mirror and seen her life laid
bare before her,
each blemish representing a day, a month, a year
each deepening line reflecting a moment of triumph or fallen tear

I am she
every woman who has learned that passion can mature and mellow
into something far greater called love,
and love on darker days can survive in unexpected ways through merely a smile,

I am me
every woman whose gender has led her to blend her sexuality
into something the world expects her to be
every woman who has been misled, used and abused, disregarded,
who has found solace in sisterhood and solidarity,
understood the greater good in unity

I am every woman who has come to know the secret.
every woman who has the confidence to repeat it .
every woman who is finally free to become the woman of strength
she was meant to be, and likes what she sees.

I am her, I am she, I am me, every woman you see.